CHICKENPOX

ELAINE LANDAU

Marshall Cavendish
Benchmark
New York

Marshall Cavendish Benchmark
99 White Plains Road
Tarrytown, New York 10591
www.marshallcavendish.us

Expert Reader: Leslie L. Barton, MD, Professor Emerita of Pediatrics,
University of Arizona College of Medicine, Tucson, Arizona

Library of Congress Cataloging-in-Publication Data

Landau, Elaine.
Chickenpox / by Elaine Landau.
p. cm.—(Head-to-toe health)
Includes bibliographical references and index.
Summary: "Provides basic information about chickenpox and its prevention"—Provided by publisher.
   ISBN 978-0-7614-3498-6
   1. Chickenpox—Juvenile literature. I. Title. II. Series.
   RC125.L35 2010
   616.9'14—dc22
   2008010782

Editor: Christine Florie
Publisher: Michelle Bisson
Art Director: Anahid Hamparian
Series Designer: Alex Ferrari

Photo Research by Candlepants Incorporated

Cover Photo: Digital Vision / Alamy Images

The photographs in this book are used by permission and through the courtesy of:
Alamy Images: Natrow Images, 4; Bubbles Photolibrary, 15; Thorsten Indra, 17; Chris Stock Photography, 23.
Photo Researchers Inc.: Dr. Linda Stannard, UCT, 7; Dr P. Marazzi, 20; Aaron Haupt, 25.
Getty Images: Bill Beatty/Visuals Unlimited, 9. *Corbis*: Owaki - Kulla, 12.

Printed in Malaysia
1 3 5 6 4 2

CONTENTS

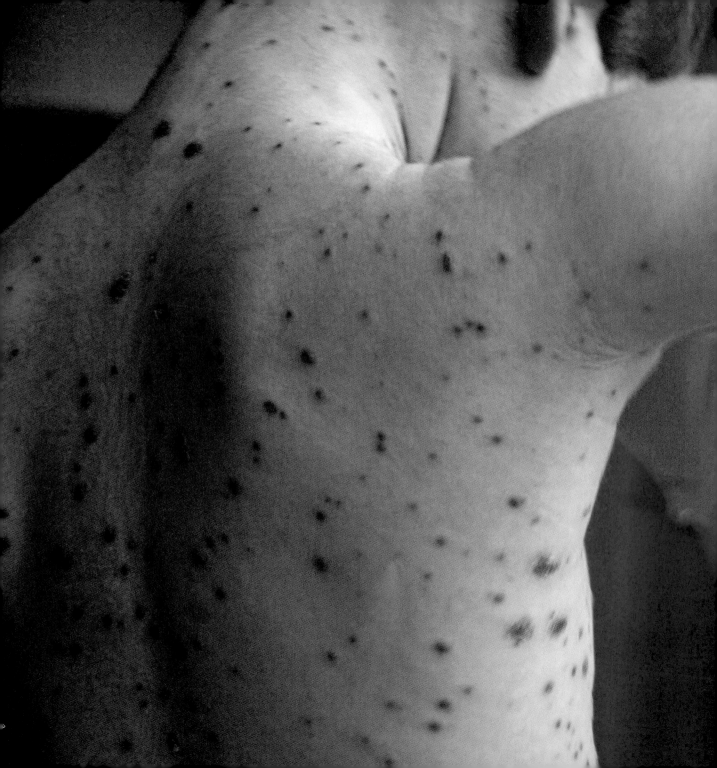

WHAT'S THAT RASH?

How did it happen? You were feeling great. Then last week you started feeling tired and achy. You didn't feel like eating and you had a headache, too.

As it turned out, you were getting sick. You found this out a day or two later when you woke up in the morning and looked in the mirror. Your face was dotted with a red rash.

The small red bumps looked a little like insect bites. Yet it wasn't summer. There weren't any creepy crawlers in your room, either. You had chickenpox.

CAN YOU CATCH CHICKENPOX FROM A CHICKEN?

The answer to that question is no! Don't let the name fool you. Chickens cannot get chickenpox. The disease only affects humans. You also cannot get chickenpox from eating chicken. So go ahead and enjoy your next chicken dinner.

◀ Chickenpox is a common childhood illness that causes itchy bumps that cover the body.

A COMMON ILLNESS

Today, chickenpox is thought of as a mild childhood disease. It usually strikes young people under fifteen years old. However, older teens and adults can also get chickenpox if they did not have it as children.

This is a book about chickenpox. It tells you all you need to know about it. If you ever get chickenpox or know someone who does, you'll understand just what's happening.

A TINY TROUBLEMAKER

Chickenpox is a disease caused by a germ known as a virus. The chickenpox virus is the varicella-zoster virus. That's a big name, but viruses are very tiny. They are so small that you need a special **microscope** to see them.

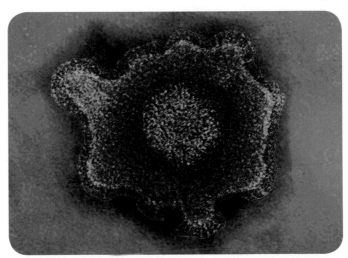

This is the virus that causes chickenpox as viewed through a high-powered microscope.

WHAT'S IT LIKE TO HAVE CHICKENPOX?

Let's face it, having chickenpox is no fun.

Some kids start feeling sick before the rash appears. They may be achy, and some have a headache, too. At times there will also be coughing.

A day or two later, there's a rash. Often it starts as groups of tiny reddish spots. First you may see these on your chest or face.

Soon the rash spreads. The spots can appear on any part of your body. You may find them on your scalp, back, arms, and legs. They may pop up between your toes and on your hands and stomach. You can even get some on your eyelids as well as in your eyes and throat.

Most kids get between 250 and 500 spots. Yet some have had over 1,500 spots. Often the illness is worse in children who have other skin conditions. It can also be worse in areas where you have a recent suntan or bad sunburn.

WHAT HAPPENS AFTER THE SPOTS SHOW UP?

The rash soon changes. The small red spots turn into raised bumps. These bumps, in turn, become **blisters**. The blisters are filled with fluid.

After a day or two, the fluid turns cloudy. Then the blisters open. Soon brown scabs form over them. Once the blisters completely heal, the scabs fall off.

All your chickenpox blisters don't appear at the same time. Just as some of the blisters form scabs, new red spots spring up elsewhere. Don't worry—this does not go on forever. The illness usually only lasts from five to ten days. Then you're as good as new again.

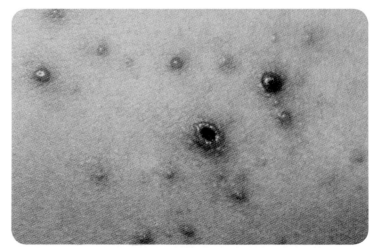

This is a close-up view of chickenpox blisters and some that are still full of fluid.

CAN YOU GET CHICKENPOX MORE THAN ONCE?

After having chickenpox, there's one thing most kids would agree on. They don't want to get it again. Happily, most of them won't.

While it is possible to get chickenpox again, it's unlikely. Your body has a built-in way to protect you from getting it a second time. Here's how it works.

When you first had chickenpox, your body sprang into action. It waged a war against the virus. It did this by making chemicals called **antibodies**.

Even after you are well, some of the antibodies remain in your body. They are like soldiers on guard in case the enemy returns. If the virus tries to invade your body again, these antibodies attack the virus. In most cases, they win the battle and you stay well. The antibodies give you a lifetime of protection.

Ick—I'm Sick!

Wow! Chickenpox is a really **contagious** disease. That means that it easily spreads from one person to another. You can pass chickenpox on to someone else before you even know you have it. That's because you are contagious a day or two before the rash appears. You remain contagious until scabs have formed on all your blisters.

You should not go to school while you're contagious, because you could end up giving your classmates chickenpox. Most kids miss between five and six days of school.

HOW LONG DOES IT TAKE BEFORE YOU START FEELING SICK?

You don't see the signs of chickenpox overnight. Let's say that you spend the day with a friend who has chickenpox. Your friend is contagious, but neither of you know it. His rash has not appeared yet.

Meanwhile, you and your friend have a great time. You share a bottle of soda and play with the same toys. Your friend coughs and sneezes, but you're not upset. It's probably just allergies, you think.

Chickenpox can spread through close contact, even though there may be no signs of infection.

The next day you feel fine. There is no hint that you have chickenpox. That's because it takes between ten and twenty-one days for the illness to develop.

HOW DO YOU GET CHICKENPOX?

There are lots of different ways to get chickenpox. Have you ever heard the saying "love is in the air"? Unfortunately, sometimes chickenpox is, too.

When a person with chickenpox coughs or sneezes, the virus is released into the air. What if you are standing next to that person? It's possible to breathe in those germs. Before you know it, you could be sick as well.

You can also get chickenpox by touching a chickenpox blister or the liquid from that blister. If you get the virus on your fingers and then touch your nose, mouth, or eyes, it can enter your body. The virus is also in

DID YOU KNOW?

Chickenpox is really contagious! Suppose someone you know gets chickenpox. Studies show that most of that person's family will also get chickenpox if they live in the same house and haven't had the disease before.

the **saliva** or spit of someone with chickenpox.

You can even get chickenpox without ever being in the same room as someone who has the disease. A contagious classmate can come to school and touch a doorknob or book that you use next. If you get the virus on your fingers, you could soon join the numbers of sick kids in your town.

THIS RASH IS ITCHY

Scratch, scratch, scratch. That's what you'll feel like doing when you have chickenpox. The rash you get is very itchy. But it's important not to scratch or pick at those blisters. Scratching can

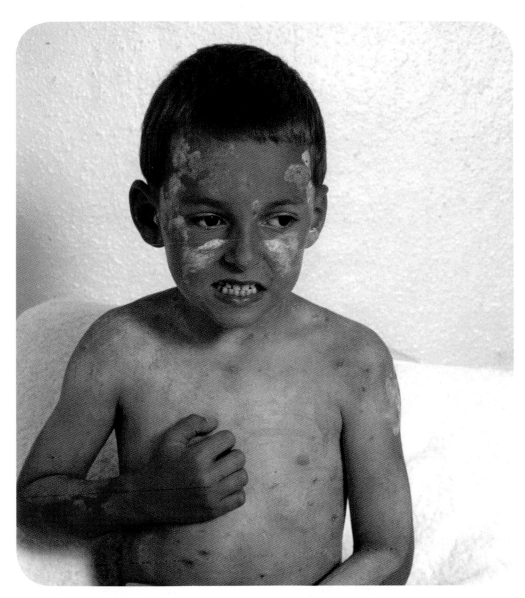

Chickenpox blisters are itchy! Don't scratch them—they can become infected and leave a scar.

tear the skin and leave you with a scar or pockmark.

There are also germs on your hands. When you scratch a broken blister, these germs can enter the sore. The blister can become **infected**.

That's why it's important to keep your fingernails clean and short when you have chickenpox. Often kids wear socks or mittens on their hands when they go to bed. This helps stop them from scratching themselves while they're asleep.

TREATING CHICKENPOX

For the most part, there isn't a lot that can be done to treat chickenpox. It is thought of as a mild illness. Usually kids aren't given medicine to combat the disease.

Yet there are some things you can do to feel better. While you are sick, it's a good idea to rest as much as you can. Cool baths and compresses sometimes help to soothe itchy skin. Some people even add uncooked oatmeal to the bath water.

Please don't try eating the oatmeal as you soak in the tub. It's not a snack. It's used to lessen itching. There are some creams and lotions that can relieve itching as well.

Fever and muscle aches are also common with chickenpox. However, you should not take aspirin. Using aspirin can

Getting rest is the best medicine for treating chickenpox.

increase a young person's chances of getting Reye syndrome. This is a serious illness that can harm the brain and liver. There are other pain relievers that don't contain aspirin that can be found at drug stores.

HAVING SHINGLES

Once you are over the chickenpox, you'll feel like your old self. You probably won't ever get the illness again. In time, you might not even remember having it.

Yet the virus isn't completely gone. Though you can't feel it, some of the virus stays in your body. In some cases, it remains quietly in your nerve cells.

Many years later it can act up again, but this time you don't get chickenpox. Instead, the virus causes a condition called shingles.

ANOTHER RASH

Like chickenpox, there's also a rash called shingles. The chickenpox rash is itchy, but the shingles rash is painful. A few days before the rash appears, there may be some early signs of the illness. You might feel some tingling or a burning feeling in certain parts of the body.

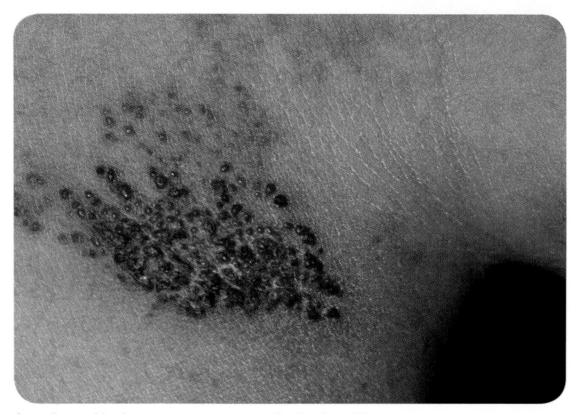

Sometimes shingles can appear years after having chickenpox.

The shingles rash starts with small red blisters. In most cases, these appear on one side of the face or body. These blisters keep forming for the next three to five days. As in chickenpox, the blisters are filled with fluid.

Before long, the blisters open and **scabs** form over them. Yet shingles tends to last longer than chickenpox.

At times, the blisters can take up to a month to heal.

Usually the pain from shingles lessens as the rash heals. However, in a small number of cases, nerve-cell pain continues for quite a while. This happens when the virus damages some of the nerve cells. But this is very rare in cases involving children.

The shingles virus tends to strike people over sixty years old, rather than young people. Each year about a million cases of shingles are reported in the United States. Unlike chickenpox, you can't "catch" shingles from someone.

WHO GETS SHINGLES?

Anyone who has ever had chickenpox can get shingles. Yet not everyone does. There is no way to tell who will develop this condition. However, you won't have to worry about this until you are much older. Studies show that half the people who reach eighty-five years of age get shingles if they've had chickenpox.

THE CHICKENPOX VACCINE

Maybe you've never had chickenpox. Having read this book, you know that you don't want to get it, either. So what's the best way to avoid the disease? Take this quick quiz to see if you're doing what you need to do.

A. You stay at least 12 feet away from your friends at all times. You also carry around a spray bottle of cleaning fluid to use on phones, doorknobs, or any shared toys.

B. You ask your parents to move to a cottage in the forest. The animals there will be your new friends. Since animals can't get chickenpox, you're safe.

C. You get the chickenpox vaccine.

What was your answer? Hopefully, it was *C*. If it was, you're on the right track!

WHAT'S A VACCINE?

A **vaccine** is a substance that protects you from a disease. It makes your body produce antibodies against the illness. These fight the germs that make you sick.

The chickenpox vaccine is given as a shot. It stops most people from getting chickenpox. Almost all of the people who get the vaccine will not get the disease.

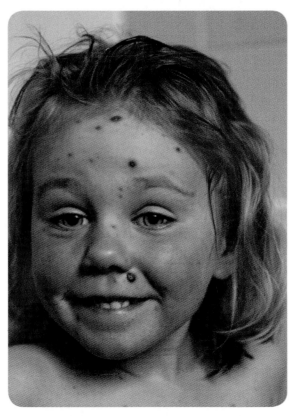

Those who do get chickenpox usually have a milder form of it. Often they get less than fifty red spots. Most won't have a fever, either.

DO WE REALLY NEED A CHICKENPOX VACCINE?

You bet we do! While chickenpox tends to be a

This toddler has a mild case of chickenpox.

mild illness, at times it can be more serious. Some people develop **severe** cases of chickenpox. These people are at greater risk of having to be hospitalized. Some have even died as a result of the illness.

There is no sure way to tell who will get a bad case of chickenpox. So it's a good idea to get the vaccine. Everyone needs two **doses** of it. The first shot should be given between twelve and fifteen months of age. The second shot should be given when the child is from four to six years old.

Teens and adults who have never had chickenpox need

two doses as well. These shots should be given between four and eight weeks apart. Pregnant women should not get the vaccine before their baby is born. That's because the effect of the vaccine on an unborn child is unknown.

The chickenpox vaccine is an important tool in the fight against chickenpox. Before the vaccine was introduced in 1995, each year

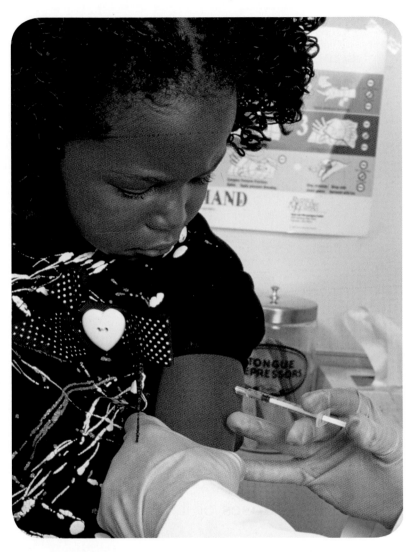

The chickenpox vaccine should be given to children between twelve and fifteen months old and again between four and six years old.

about 11,000 people in the United States landed in the hospital because of this disease. About one hundred people in the United States even died of chickenpox each year.

Things are different now. Today, most children in the United States have been vaccinated. They've taken a big step toward staying well. Hopefully, one day even fewer people will get chickenpox.

Glossary

antibodies — substances made by your body to fight disease

blisters — closed sores that fill with liquid

contagious — a disease that is easily spread

dose — a measured amount of medicine

infected — to have an illness caused by germs

microscope — an instrument used to make small things look larger

parasite — a germ that cannot live outside the human body
   for very long

saliva — a clear liquid in your mouth

scab — the hard crust that forms over a wound as it heals

severe — serious or dangerous

vaccine — a substance given to protect you from a disease

FIND OUT MORE

BOOKS

Boudreau, Gloria. *The Immune System*. San Diego, CA: Kidhaven Press, 2004.

Goldstein, Natalie. *Viruses*. New York: Rosen, 2004.

Nye, Bill. *Bill Nye the Science Guy's Great Big Book of Tiny Germs*. New York: Hyperion, 2005.

Royston, Angela. *Staying Healthy*. Chicago: Raintree, 2004.

Sherman, Josepha. *The War Against Germs*. New York: Rosen, 2004.

DVDS

Stone House Productions. *Health for Children*. Wynnewood, PA: Schlessinger Media, 2005.

Tapestry International Productions. *Understanding Viruses*. Bethesda, MD: Discovery Communications, 2004.

WEB SITES

Chickenpox

www.kidshealth.org/kid/health_problems/infection/chicken_pox.html

Visit this Web site for some interesting and helpful information about chickenpox.

Infection, Detection, Protection

www.amnh.org/nationalcenter/infection/infectionindex.html

Check out this Web site to meet the microbes that can make you sick.

You'll also learn ways to stay well.

INDEX

Page numbers in **boldface** are illustrations.

ABOUT THE AUTHOR

Award-winning author Elaine Landau has written more than three hundred books for young readers. Many of these are on health and science topics. For Marshall Cavendish, Landau has written *Asthma; Bites and Stings; Broken Bones; Bumps, Bruises, and Scrapes; Cavities and Toothaches*; and *The Common Cold* for the Head-to-Toe Health series.

Landau received a bachelor's degree in English and journalism from New York University and a master's degree in library and information science from Pratt Institute. You can visit Elaine Landau at her Web site: www.elainelandau.com.